MW01230822

ANXIETY IN RELATIONSHIP

The Essential guide to Overcome Anxiety, Jealousy and Negative Thinking. Heal Your Insecurity and Attachment to Establish Relationships Without Couple Conflicts.

By

Elliott J. Power

TABLE OF CONTENTS

CHAPTER 1
INTRODUCTION

Many individuals experience a kind of long, drawn-out, chronic anxiety with which they live each day. This type of anxiety reduces the quality of life. Still, it is manageable because it rarely gets too intense and instead provides this persistent unease feeling, which takes away from your daily activities.

Love is probably the most powerful emotion possible. It is not uncommon for it to profoundly impact your relationship and your quality of life when you start experiencing anxiety over that love. Anxiety in relationships is complex and means different things to different people, but there is no denying that you will do anything you can to stop it once you have it.

There is nothing that keeps a relationship strong and safe better than understanding. Many become more acquainted with communication and the various ways we can connect once proven communication is formed.

When contact includes talking to our families, friends, individuals in general, when things are not going so well in their relationship, individuals tend to turn to their others first (partner, spouse, friends, etc.).

With that in mind, it has more to do with you managing your relationship anxiety than it does with them, and you can't expect them to contribute. The following are fundamental techniques to ensure that your relationship will recover.

CHAPTER 2
UNDERSTANDING ANXIETY IN YOUR RELATIONSHIP

W hat is the "anxiety around relationships," and why do certain people have it?

When either or both individuals in the relationship spend more time worrying anxiously about the relationship than turning toward the relationship itself.

Expectations may differ, but awkward thoughts are the same. A fear of rejection, feeling as though they care more, a constant fear of infidelity or an overall apprehension of the stability of the relationship contributes to a lack of confidence.

There are several reasons why you might have anxiety about a relationship. Manipulative spouses may have set the tone for potential anxieties: parent attachments, abusive exes, poor communication, and ineffective therapy as causes.

An individual with anxiety about relationships doesn't always have a partner that isn't trust worthy but if you don't voice your worries and desires, your significant other may very well be just living their lives, utterly unaware of your concerns "Any conduct that causes one partner to doubt the other at the same time creates conflict. Secretive conversations, text messages, micro-cheating, and failure to communicate with your partner can spike fear."

Similarly, when you don't feel your best and most comfortable, your anxiety could skyrocket. "The game of comparison and contrast fosters anxiety that your relationship isn't as good as others, and causes nervous thoughts to grow as you ruminate why your relationship isn't as 'successful' as others." That's all imagination, of course.

ANXIETY IN RELATIONSHIP IS NATURAL

If you're in a long-term, committed relationship or fresh off a Tinder swiping session, anxiety about relationships can – and will definitely – pop up anywhere.

Whether it is due to lack of confidence, fear of rejection, questioning the compatibility, or worrying about non-reciprocal feelings, most people are experiencing some sort of discomfort about their partner's future. The real issue occurs when everyday worries turn into deteriorating tension or result in self-sabotage that hurts your relationship.

Anxiety about relationships can cause people to indulge in habits that end up driving away their partner.

The first step to maintaining it at a manageable level is to recognize that some anxiety is entirely natural.

When you start seeing things spiraling out of control — and have ripple effects that start affecting your relationship and your mental health — here's what you need to know about finding the cause and keeping it under control.

SIGNS THAT YOUR RELATIONSHIP ANXIETY HAS REACHED AN ALARMING DEGREE

"It's important to remember that everybody has some anxiety about relationships, and that's to be expected," said Dr. Amanda Zayde, a clinical psychologist. "However, if you find yourself hyper-vigilant for signs that something is wrong, or if you encounter recurrent anxiety that affects your everyday life, please take some time to fix it. All in their relationships needs to feel safe and connected."

Not only is this constant state of mind psychologically draining and harmful to your health, but it can also eventually lead to the disintegration of the relationship.

"The uncertainty about relationships can cause people to participate in activities that end up driving their partner away," Dr. Zayde says. "To call 20 times in a row, leap to conclusions, or become emotionally detached, for example. It can also cause immense anxiety and frustration because people spend hours trying to decipher the actions of their partner".

Dr. Forshee continues, "They may bother with social media accounts of their lover, google them incessantly or have their friends assist in doing some research. They may wrongly accuse their new lover of things they have no proof for, or become excessively clingy, just to fulfill the desire for euphoria and attachment".

Although these behaviors can cause fear or anxiety to decline for the moment through mini-neurochemical bursts, Forshee says, they're just a short-term diversion. You have to do some intense, inner searching for the long-term easement, and then work proactively to reduce the anxiety. And this step begins by discovering the actual reason behind the primary cause of the anxiety.

Childhood: Root Cause of Anxiety in Relationship

"Relationship anxiety also arises from patterns of attachment, which form in early childhood," Zayde says. "A child builds a blueprint of what to expect from others based on their experiences in early care."

She says that a child can learn to either communicate or inhibit his or her emotional and physical needs, depending on the exactness and quality of the caregiver's response. This coping mechanism may work at the time, but when extended to adult, intimate relationships, it may turn into maladaptive behaviors.

Sometimes, anxiety about relationships stems from patterns of attachment that grow in early childhood.

A typical example of maladaptive behavior is what psychologists term an enmeshed relationship, or a situation in which a parent is excessively involved in the life of a child, as described in the book of Greenberg, Cicchetti, and Cummings, Attachment in the Years of the Preschool. This can result in "reciprocally invasive, controlling conduct," and "a great deal of uncertainty and anxiety on both sides over the actual or threatened separation."

For those who feel easily suffocated in a relationship, on the flip side, they may have had childhood experiences, which caused them to avoid relationships and bonding. For example, a child with an inattentive parent may learn to suppress their inherent tenderness towards bonding to escape heartache and rejection feelings. As an adult, the child can have a difficult time committing to a relationship or being insecure in it.

If this is true to your experience, it may be worth looking further into attachment theory, which has profoundly influenced the way relationship experts and contemporary psychologists think of relationships. You can also use a questionnaire to decide what kind of relationship style you and your partner have.

Your Ex Might be the Blame for Your Anxiety

Besides your upbringing, past relationships can also play a role in the relationships you act in.

"When you experience the kind of relationship anxiety that you fear being cheated on or lack of faith in your new admirer, this might result from past relationship interactions embedded within your brain. Our brain will never forget", Forshee said. "The brain circuitry has become conditioned to connect those characteristics, smells, sounds, and emotions with previous memories of a lover and relationship. Your brain has developed a powerful pattern from previously acquired experiences, and your brain maintains remnants of that circuitry, even after you have fallen for someone new."

Finally, the body releases massive quantities of strong chemicals like oxytocin, dopamine, cortisol, and vasopressin when you start a new relationship. When combined, these "heart chemicals" make bonding and engagement more accessible. While they make us feel very passionate, they can also make us feel emotionally unstable, insecure, and obsessed with new partners. When we're around our partners — especially when we embrace, kiss, or have sex — this development of hormones goes into overdrive.

"When we're away from our new love, are afraid of rejection, or are rejected, it can make us feel like we're going through the withdrawal of addiction," Forshee explained, which can lead to unhealthy obsession and fear.

HOW TO CONQUER ANXIETY IN RELATIONSHIP

It's maybe the simple part to find the root causes of your relationship anxiety. Although it can be gradual and daunting to conquer your fear, it can be achieved if you are consciously conscious, thoroughly committed to change, and be kind to yourself as you walk the road ahead.

"Take some time to understand better how your early experiences have influenced your relationship style, and remain mindful of ways you can replicate early experiences with your new partner," Zayde suggests. "Pay attention to how much you leap to conclusions, and whether or not you have enough evidence to support your concerns; sometimes, our concerns are focused on past experiences, not our present relationship."

Follow these expert tips to remain in control and help relieve anxiety as anxious thoughts begin to grab hold:

- Running. Forshee suggests hitting the gym to help alleviate the tension at the moment. Various studies have shown that exercise improves the development and release of serotonin. The two worst things you can do are isolating yourself and being physically stagnant, so get going.

- Healthy self-talk. "Engage in constructive self-talking rather than negative self-talking, and help a friend remind you of happier days and what the good things are now in your life," Forshee says. "This act helps to increase the development of serotonin in the anterior cingulate cortex, which is a part of your brain right behind the frontal areas responsible for treatment, judgment, and impulse control."

- Take a step back. In feeling nervous, Forshee emphasizes the importance of not acting on your emotional impulses. She says your brain won't let you make wise decisions in the heat of the moment, and you're most likely going to regret your actions soon afterward.

- Find ways to unwind. "If you are unable to get assistance from your support team or are unable to move, it could be useful to engage in a calming technique such as diaphragm breathing. This can help with physiological de-escalation so that you can think more clearly and feel less worked up, "says Forshee.

- Take aid. "Finally, if you notice that your relationship anxiety has taken over in a way that you believe is beyond your control — or has wrought havoc in your life — it's likely to be helpful to pursue professional therapy."

Ultimately, managing relationship anxiety depends on gaining control of the feelings and mental process. There's a strong connection between your wellbeing — and the quality of your relationship — and the level of knowledge you have about yourself, your attitudes, and your feelings. Take action to recognize the causes of anxiety and re-route the cycle it incites today, and you might just be able to create a new path for your brain to follow around next time.

HOW TO OVERCOME RELATIONSHIP ANXIETY

Relationships can be one of the planet's most pleasurable things ... but they can also be a fertile ground for negative thoughts and emotions. Anxiety about relationships can occur at almost any stage of the courtship. Just thinking about being in a relationship will bring up stress for many single people. The early stages will present them with endless worries if and when people start dating: "Does he/she like me?" "Is this going to work out?" "What is this serious?". Unfortunately, in the later stages of a marital relationship, these issues do not appear to subside. Indeed, as things get closer to a couple, anxiety can become even more severe. Thoughts rush in like this: "Will this last?" "Do I like him/her?" "Should we hesitate?" "Am I ready for this kind of engagement?" "Does he/she lose interest?". All this thinking about our relationships can cause us to feel very lonely.

It can give us reason to separate ourselves from our partners. Our anxiety at its worst can even drive us to give up on love altogether. Knowing more about the causes and consequences of stress about relationships will help us recognize the negative thoughts and behaviors that can undermine our love lives. How do we keep our fear in check and get vulnerable to those we love? What triggers anxiety about Relationships?

Simply put, falling in love surprises us in ways we don't expect.

The more we love another, the more we are to lose. We become scared of getting hurt in several ways, both conscious and unconscious. To a certain extent, we all have a fear of being close. Ironically, this anxiety always shows up when we get exactly what we want when we experience love like we never have or are handled in different ways. When we move into a partnership, it's not just the things that happen between our partner that make us anxious; it's the stuff about what's going on that we say ourselves.

The "powerful inner voice" is a phrase used to describe the mean coach we all have in our heads who criticizes us, imposes bad advice on us, and fuels our fear of intimacy. It is that which tells us:

"You are too ugly/fat/boring to maintain an interest in yourself."

"You are never going to meet anyone, so why even try it?" "You can't believe him."

"He is looking for a better guy" "She has no real love for you."

Get out before it hurts you. This vital voice inside makes us turn against ourselves and the people who are close to us.

It can encourage aggressive, pessimistic, and suspicious thinking that lowers our self-esteem and induces unhealthy levels of mistrust, defensiveness, envy, and anxiety. It effectively feeds us with a steady stream of thoughts that ruins our happiness and makes us worry about our relationship, rather than just enjoy it. When we get into our minds, dwelling on those worrying feelings, we get too disconnected from our partner's real relationship.

We can begin to behave in negative ways, to make nasty comments, or to become childish or parental towards our significant others. Imagine your partner staying at work late in one night, for instance. Seated alone at home, your inner critic begins to tell you, "Where is she? Could you believe it? Possibly she wants to be separated from you. She is trying to avoid you. She no longer loves you." These feelings will snowball in your mind until you feel nervous, angry, or anxious by the time your partner gets home. You could be acting angry or cold, then set off your partner to feel irritated and defensive. Soon, you changed the dynamic between yourself completely. Instead of enjoying the time you have with each other, you might be wasting a whole night feeling distant and angry. Now the gap you initially feared was effectively forced. The culprit behind this prophecy, which fulfills itself, is not the situation itself. It's that vital inner voice that warped your thought, skewed your perceptions, and eventually led you down a destructive path.

We are much more robust than we realize when it comes to all of the things we worry about ourselves in relationships. In reality, we're able to cope with the hurts and rejections we fear so much. We can feel pain and ultimately cure. But our vital voice inside tends to terrorize and catastrophize reality. It can stir up severe anxiety spells about non-existent complexities and risks that are not even observable. Even when important things happen, someone breaks up with us or has an interest in somebody else; our vital inner voice is going to tear us apart in ways that we don't deserve. It will distort reality entirely and weaken our power and resilience. It is this pessimistic roommate who is still offering lousy advice. That you cannot survive. Just put your guard up and never make someone else weak.

We form defenses and hear influential voices based on our own specific experiences and adaptations. Some of us tend to become clingy and insecure in our acts when we feel nervous or uncertain. In response, we may feel possessive or controlling towards our partner. Inversely, some of us in our relationships would feel easily intruded on. We withdraw from our partners and detach ourselves from our feelings of desire. We may act aloof, distant, or guarded. These relating trends may come from our early styles of attachment. Our pattern of attachment is formed in our extensions to childhood and continues to serve as a working model for adult relationships. It affects how each of us is reacting to our needs and how we are going to fulfill them. Different types of attachment may cause us to feel different degrees of anxiety about the relationship. You will learn more about your kind of passion and how it affects your romantic relationships here.

What thoughts are perpetuating tension in the relationship?

The unique critical inner voices that we have about ourselves, our spouses, and relationships are created by the early attitudes to which we have been exposed in our family or society at large. Cultural assumptions, as well as behaviors our influential caretakers have about themselves and others, will invade our perspective and shade our current perceptions. Although the inner critic of all is different, some familiar critical voices within include:

- Relevant Voices inside the Partnership.

- Only wind people up getting hurt.

- Never do marriages work out.

- Your Partner Voices.

- Men are so arrogant, incompetent, and egotistical.

- Women are so delicate, so weak, and so indirect.

- He only wants to be with friends of his.

- Why get so excited? What's so sweet of her anyway?

- Possibly, he cheats on you.

- You can't believe her.

- He just can't get it right.

- Voices for Yourself.

- You'll never find anyone else who knows you.

- Don't get too hooked on her.

- He doesn't care for you.

- She's too good for you.

- You have to maintain an interest in him.

- You're better off alone.

- She will ignore you until she gets to know you.

- You have to have the leverage.

- If he gets angry, it is your fault.

- Don't be too weak, or actually get hurt.

HOW DOES ANXIETY AFFECT US IN RELATIONSHIP

When we shed light on our history, we quickly recognize many early factors influenced our pattern of attachment, our psychological defenses, and our vital voice inside. All these factors contribute to our uncertainty about relationships and can lead us in many ways to sabotage our love lives.

Having to hear our inner critic and giving in to that fear can lead to the following actions:

Cling - Our propensity to behave aggressively towards our partner could be when we feel nervous. When we entered the relationship, we may stop feeling like the independent, influential people we were. As a consequence, we can easily fall apart, behave jealously or dangerously, or no longer participate in separate activities.

Control - We can try to dominate or influence our partner when we feel threatened. We should lay down rules about what they can and can't do just to relieve our feelings of fear or anxiety. This action can alienate our partner and make us feel resentful.

Reject - If we are uncertain about our relationship, it is aloofness that is one of the defenses we can turn to. To defend ourselves or to beat our partner to the punch, we may become cold or refuse. These acts can be subtle or explicit, but in our partner, it is almost always a sure way to cause distance or build vulnerability.

Withhold - Often, we prefer to withhold from our partner when we feel nervous or scared, as opposed to outright rejection. Maybe things got close, and we feel stirred, so we withdraw. We hold back little affections or give up entirely on any part of our relationship. It may seem like a passive act to withhold, but it is one of the quietest desire and attraction killers in a relationship.

Punish - Our reaction to our distress is often more violent, and we are merely punishing, taking our feelings out on our partner. We-shout and scream or give the cold shoulder to our partner. It's essential to be mindful of how much our acts are a response to our partner and how much they are a response to our vital voice inside.

Withdraw - We can give up real acts of love and intimacy when we feel scared in a relationship and withdraw into a "fantasy bond." A fantasy bond is an illusion of attachment that replaces real acts of love. In this fantasy state, we concentrate on shape over substance. We will stay in the relationship to feel safe but give up on the essential parts of the relationship. In a bond of illusion, we frequently indulge in many of the above described detrimental behaviors as a way of creating distance and protecting ourselves against the discomfort that inevitably comes with feeling free and in love.

CHAPTER 3
DOUBT CAUSED BY ANXIETY IN RELATIONSHIP

The relationship doubt you should not ignore

Even though we love our partners to the moon and back, it is always possible to find ourselves facing questions that make it challenging to communicate. From confusion about your shared objectives to a total contact divide — once our suspicions start to fester, letting them go can be challenging.

If we want to avoid the breakup of our relationships, we have to discuss our suspicions and the root causes behind them. Although some doubts come to any couple usually and naturally, others are signs of alarm that should not be ignored. Don't wait for heartbreak and tension to come knocking at your door. Try to fix now to get to the root of problems surrounding your relationship before they overtake the affection you have for each other

Doubts are a prominent part of the process.

No matter who you are, and no matter how long your relationship has withstood the tests of time — you've faced questions about your partnership at one point or another. When it comes to our romantic relationships, items are a standard part of the process, but some are more detrimental to our peace of mind and health than others. When faced with questions, we've got to answer them and be truthful about where they're taking root.

Running from our questions leaves us nothing but afraid, weakened, and hanging on to something that might not be right. Although doubts are natural and come with the seasons of our relationships, some doubts are also critical red flags that need to be addressed to sustain and safeguard our inner peace and long-term wellbeing.

To overcome the questions, we have to answer them frankly and fiercely. That's not just about questioning our friends. It means facing ourselves and the burdens we are bearing, as well as the stuff from this life and our relationships that we want. Addressing those questions can be a moment of change for you and your family. Avoid running out of the items and reach out to learn. It's the only way you can find your way to the reality you must both know.

WHERE DOUBT COME FROM IN OUR RELATIONSHIP

Romantic doubts are natural, and they come and go no matter what stage you find yourself in your relationship. However, they have underlying causes, and these causes may also be just as significant as the same doubts. To ensure that our fears are rooted in the right place, we must first consider where they come from.

Stressful Atmosphere

Stress is a major toxin in our surroundings, and it is one of the most probable. We are living in a chaotic world, and it creates utter chaos when the stress rains over our lives. We also get into a state of constant anticipation of the worst as a way of preparing ourselves for the challenges. The more tension we face, the more questions we find ourselves grappling within our personal lives. However, these suspicions are always our problems in disguise — so check your stress levels to see if there is something you do to self-sabotage.

Unresolved Baggage

Our unresolved emotional baggage is perhaps the most common cause of romantic doubts. Our past pain plays an essential part in our future, as it moves from relationship to relationship around us. You have to work through the traumas of your past marriages, and even your childhood, to make sure you will later lead a safe, happy relationship. If you still hold your past baggage, this may lead you to doubt the legitimacy of your right here and now.

External Pressure

Often it's the outer world that contributes to the suspicions within our relationships that we experience. Society goes a long way to help us form our views on everything from how we dress up to how we create relationships. If your relationship has a lot of pressure from friends and family (or even your career) to deal with — then it may lead to some serious questions that follow you around. To prevent such problems, we need to be clear about what we as individuals want, rather than simply falling in line with the herd.

Off-mark Validation

Are you anyone who gets approval from outside sources? Besides being a significant indicator of vulnerability, it can also become a source of severe doubts about the relationship. The more you base your worth off the people and interactions around you, the more unpredictable and dysfunctional you will become your inner self, your ability to make eroding decisions, and you will come to doubt everything ... including your ability to make decisions on the most basic levels.

Bad Partner Choices

Like it or not — we always question our partners because we choose the wrong guy/gal. At times, our reservations are the way our subconscious brain tells us that the relationship (and the person who shares it with us) is a bad match. It's up to us to wake up in those moments and decide if this is the actual reality we're missing. Everything else may seem right in your relationship, but if something still feels wrong — it is wrong. More often than not, listen to your gut.

Lack of Nurturing

Although you may be with the right person, you might still find yourself grappling with doubts — even if you may have both worked hard to overcome your baggage. It may mean a lack of nurturing that feeds an increasing divide when things are still not working out (or the doubts are creeping in). Relationships are living beings breathing in and of themselves, and they take a great deal of energy and commitment for all interested parties.

Doubts, you can never forget

So, is there a seething of doubt in your relationship? Don't forget these. Of course, as they might be, whether you stop them or disregard them, they always bear implications. Stop running from those worries and face them in the back of your mind. These are the questions you can never in any conditions ignore about your relationship.

Am I being drawn to them?

One of the most common relationship doubts to experience deals in our level of physical and emotional attraction. For a connection to succeed in some long-term sense, all partners need to feel a general attraction to each other. This draw can fluctuate through the physical and emotional planes, but it should still have its available pull in place. Although it's normal to challenge your attraction from time to time, you should always take serious doubts ... well, really.

Am I Humiliated?

If you have to ask yourself if your partner is manipulating you — some questions need to be answered. We should be able to trust our partners, and we should be mindful that even though we are out of the picture, they have our backs. If your partner makes a fool out of you whenever you're not around, or you're humiliated continuously by foolish behavior, then you have to fix your questions about them and make sure they're a person you can live around.

She/he is loyal?

Loyalty is crucial in every relationship, but when it comes to our romantic relationships, it becomes particularly important. The incredibly critical thing is to question the loyalty of your partner. In comparison to confidence, commitment implies the willingness of the other individual to stand by your side through hardship. In contrast, it may also indicate their ability to hold you back from the attacks of others. It's hard to trust your partner without commitment. It's also challenging to make sure you'll always be there to help each other when the chips fall where they can.

What if the beliefs that we carry are too different?

Values form who we are and direct us towards people and experiences that can bring value and pleasure to our lives. We are rudderless in a stormy sea, without our principles. Without ideals in a relationship, we can find ourselves clashing with frustrated expectations and behaviors that are not balanced. Doubting your partner's principles is something we can never ignore. It is a warning sign that things are not what they look like.

Want the same stuff?

While many of us have been brought up to believe it's the similarities that have sustained good relationships, the real glue in a long-term partnership wants the same things out of life. It makes it easier to resolve challenges and concentrate on one another and our dreams when we want the same things from our futures as our partners do. But it becomes easier to find disappointment when we seek different things. Do you want something the same as your partner does? This is a grave doubt to carry in your heart.

Are they loyal to me?

Honesty in a relationship is vital, no matter what age or stage you are in. We need to be truthful with each other to trust each other, and we need to be honest in ensuring integrity and transparency. A partner who isn't honest with you is one who gives their personal interests priority over your own. It's natural to distrust someone you can't trust, but it shouldn't be a regular part of your relationship.

How big is it that they make me feel?

Our friends and spouses need to pick us up and inspire us while we are down or dealing with life's difficulty. Besides that, they should always treat us with compassion and reverence. Without that, keeping a just relationship is unlikely. If your partner makes you feel weak, inferior, or otherwise insignificant — then soon, the doubts begin to fester. You're going to doubt yourself, but you're going to challenge them as well. As well as someone else's thoughts on the world around you.

Then what you have to do

Did you decide the doubts are simply too much to bear? These are the steps that you need to take next to resolve your concerns and find peace. The longer you run out of receiving the answers that you need, the greater the pain. Don't wait until the conflict is getting bigger. Face your fears to rediscover your truth, and address your doubts.

1. Consider which source

In addressing your doubts, the first step is to consider the source. While some of our doubts are well-founded or justified, others are simply projections of our doubts. We have to dig deep and be brutally honest about where our concerns come from. We need to look at the source of our doubts and get real about the reasons we have come to see our partner in another light.

Break down your doubts one by one, and work backward to get to the root of your relationship's arrival. Don't shy away from past pain and baggage, and don't lie when you make comparisons that don't exist.

Know that your partner isn't your dysfunctional parent; they aren't the ex who broke your heart into a million pieces. Analyze the comparisons you make and know when to spot the projection signs. Ask critical questions for yourself. Doubts about my partner? Or do I put my past in doubt? Is this a behavior that they have shown to me? Or am I looking back for yesterday's troubles? Once you are aware of where your doubts come from, you take steps to correct them.

2. Get yourself clear about what you want

Once you've identified your doubts and sussed out what's real and what's not, you need to be clear about what you want so you can create an action plan. Consider what it means most to you in this world and what you hope to build 5, 10, or even 20 years from now before you open up to your partner or make any dramatic moves.

Take yourself a few quiet moments each day and spend some time journaling about what you want from your life. Consider every aspect of your life, from your career to where you want to live, to your family. Look at your relationship and compare it with your dream partnership. Is this that person with whom you can build tomorrow?

Don't hurry the process and avoid any truths that are required. If you're standing on the edge of a cliff looking at a relationship with more questions than advantages, you need to be sure about what you want to do before you cut any cords that you don't want to. Accept your needs at face value and see you need them to be happy.

3. Open up to each other

It's time to open up to your partner with your truths to hand, and have an honest discussion of your concerns. Again, this is a process that can not be hurried and one that should be carried out with special care. That means you have a grasp on what you want, what you need, and the emotions that surround the issues you have. With little less than the facts, there's no point running into a big conversation.

Find a safe space where you and your partner can securely open up to each other, without fear of being overheard or disrupted. Choose the time you carefully talk to each other and make sure it's not in the midst of a lot of emotional distress or chaos.

Open to your partner. Explain to them your doubts and explain the work you have done to get to this point. Leave off any accusing language and try (as much as possible) to keep your emotions out of it. Give them space and time to answer once you have had a chance to express yourself. Remember that this is not necessarily a one-and-done conversation, too. If you need to, walk away but don't stop talking until both of you get answers.

4. Check your space.

Now that all is out in the open, it's time to lean into the room, separating you and your partner. With your new information, you both need time to process how you feel, and you need time to weigh the information against your needs and action plans. How you feel when you give up your doubts can differ significantly from how you feel after expressing your partner's needs and hearing their answer.

Make yourself comfortable spending time and get back into the routines and pastimes that bring you joy. Investigate who you are more thoroughly and re-engage with life in a way that gives you a more in-depth, more compassionate viewpoint.

Our doubts can be natural moments of fear and passing, but they can also be important indicators that we are moving in the wrong way. If your doubts are yet to subside, then you need to spend some time in your world — to decide if that's preferable to a world shared with someone else. Once again, the key here is honesty... uncomfortable as it might be. Explore who you are, and actively and without hesitation, explore what you want from your life.

5. Talk the patterns

Sometimes, our doubts arise because of concrete patterns that repeatedly rear their heads. These patterns manifest as self-sabotage, in which we drive away people who might otherwise fit well into our lives and futures. To stop them, we have to address these patterns, and then quench the originating fire that feeds them. This means digging through our pastures and hearts to let go of the pain that lurks in the shadows.

It is time to address any patterns that might feed your negative emotions and thoughts after you have both addressed your concerns and given yourself time and space to explore and process them. You need to be brutally honest here, once again. Do you doubt the ability of your partner to be there for you? Or are you pushing away someone you don't believe deserves?

Look at the way your past relationships have played out. What stopped you opening up? What's broadening the divides? Is it old wounds from your childhood, playing your heart's stage time and time again? Do you prove right to your dismissive and narcissistic parents by failing in love, just as they have? Go back as far as necessary to get to the root of your patterns. Stop shooting yourself in your foot and begin to let go of the baggage that pushes love out of your life.

Putting everything together...

Our relationships are a significant cornerstone of our lives, but they can fill us with fear and doubt as well. When these doubts appear in our partnerships, we need to address them so that we can see them for what they truly are. The more we approach the next steps with compassion and understanding the better for our relationship After all, the only way to tackle your doubts is by opening to your partner and taking action.

Take some time to consider the source of your doubts or fears before making any bold moves. The way we feel about a situation, sometimes, is justified. But other times, it's just a manifestation of our baggage from the past. Get clear about where your worries come from, then (once you know their source) spend some time familiarizing yourself with what you need and want from life. With this knowledge to hand, you can approach your partner and open yourself to some honest dialogue, which will help both of you find the resolution you need. Once both of you have said what you need to say, take some time (and space) to process your feelings and next action plans. Address whatever negative patterns come into play. Take charge, and stand up for the things you want and need. You are the only one that can be, after all.

CHAPTER 4
THE INSECURE FEELING

It can be excruciating and upsetting to feel insecure in your relationship. It can manifest in all manner of ways. You may feel like your partner is always about to break up with you. You may have difficulty trusting them not to cheat on you. Or you might think that your connection has become weaker and weaker for a while and that the foundations are starting to fall away.

Feeling like this can make it hard to have a great deal of faith in your future together-and can sometimes leave you wondering whether breaking up would be the easiest solution. Also, it can start having adverse effects in other areas of your life. It can undermine your self-esteem and confidence, and this can make it difficult to feel able to address any issues.

WHERE INSECURITY ORIGINATES FROM

A sense of insecurity can stem from several different places in your relationship.

If you and your partner have not been effectively communicating about issues or making an effort to maintain your connection, you may start feeling as if you are drifting apart.

Insecurity can also be a consequence of changes in your relationship. For example, if you have moved in together or married recently, you may feel all sorts of new strains and pressures. If you can't discuss these together, then you can start feeling less confident about your ability to work as a team.

It can also come from self-image or self-esteem issues. For example, if you feel exceptionally low after having put on weight after a series of disappointments in your work life or less happy with your physical appearance, this could make you worry about your relationship.

Sometimes we can carry feelings from past relationships into our current relationship-including those with family members. If we weren't having very secure or loving relationships when we were younger with our parents or primary caregivers, we might be carrying that feeling with us as adults. Past romantic relationships where your trust has been broken can make it hard to trust anybody else. You may find yourself searching for 'patterns' or assuming history will repeat itself.

What to do to tackle insecurity?

The first call is to talk things over together. This can be tricky, of course-especially if you haven't been talking correctly for a while or you feel hurt or angry with your partner.

If you do feel capable, however, you might find the following tips helpful:

Keep things laid back. Hearing the words 'we must talk' can make a defensive feeling even for the most laid back person! The more positive framing of things can get things off to a better start. You may want to try something like, 'I really would like to talk to you about our relationship when you have a chance.'

Choose the right moment. Try talking when things go well and not ill. Bringing things up amid an argument can only create more conflict. If you introduce the subject when you feel good about the relationship, both of you are more likely to move in a positive direction.

Tell how you feel, not how you think they're making you feel. If both of you are merely trading blows and blaming each other for everything, you probably won't get anywhere. To keep things under control, it can be useful to use phrases about 'I' ('I sometimes feel worried about that') rather than names about 'you' ('you always make me feel worried because').

Listen. Even if it's hard to hear what your partner has to say, try and stick with it. For it to work, a conversation needs to go both ways. Try to start by recognizing their perspective can be different from yours.

You might even plan. It may sound a bit clinical, but it may be useful to think about what you want to say in advance. That doesn't mean drawing up a shopping list of grievances but merely collecting your thoughts about what you want to talk about.

Come on to it again. Rarely in one chat are these things solved. Working on relationship issues takes time and effort, so you may need to revisit things in a month to see how you're getting on with each other. This kind of conversation will seem far less appalling after a while!

7 STEPS IN YOUR RELATIONSHIP TO OVERCOMING INSECURITIES

"The most common insecurity people bring into relationships is that they're 'not enough'—not sexy enough, not pretty enough, not thin enough, not sufficiently successful—all have to do with not being sufficient," explains Terri Orbuch, professor at Oakland University in Michigan, Institute for Social Research.

That said, insecurities can – and do – run the gamut, Some common ones:

- Doubt that long-term relationships can be healthy and satisfying. As in, you're worried that your partner won't love the "real you" once the shininess of a new relationship wears off (Or vice versa.)

- Worrying about goals, expectations, and values changing or inconsistent with the relationship. Thoughts you may experience: What if they decide they don't want to have children? What if we can't agree where we should be living?

- Fearing your partner would suddenly give you up. This one is more common if you have an edgy style of attachment that usually stems from what you observed about growing relationships and how your parents responded to your needs.

So yeah, having insecurities in relationships is normal, but being obsessed with them will not do you or your partner any good.

Instead, try this 7-step, expert-approved process to avoid sabotaging your bond by hang-ups:

1. Stop assuming you are to blame for your insecurities.

... Or they are your partner. Insecurities aren't just pop-up from nowhere. According to Orbuch, they are often triggered by specific events, people, ex-partners, or even current partners.

Because you can't control all of that (especially, you know, others), focus on what you can control: yourself. The first step to tackling your insecurities head-on is to let go of self-blame and self-bashing.

Think you're the only one to have insecurity? Not even near. Celebrities also have them.

2. Curiosity tackles your insecurities.

Forget all the defense mechanisms that you used to survive the three-year middle school insecurity fest. Now you are an adult, meaning it's time to have your doubts.

According to Squyres, the best way to do that is by viewing them with curiosity and an open mind.

Spend time specifying exactly why you don't think you're enough. ("My first boyfriend cheated me so; I don't have what it takes to keep people interested in the long haul.")

Evaluating where your insecurities come from (write them down so you can see them as a third party if you need them) will help you figure out if they are truth-based or simply fear-based.

You will see most (if not all) of the time; this is the latter one.

3. Let your partner know how you feel.

If your S.O. isn't a mind reader (spoiler alert: they aren't), you need to tell them when you feel insecure — and encourage them to do the same for you.

"A safe emotional space creates a strong foundation for a loving relationship with your partner."

"A safe emotional space with your partner, where you know you can directly but gently discuss worries, creates a strong foundation for a loving, trusting relationship," says Squyres.

This can be harder if the behavior of your partner triggers your insecurities, of course, but that is when it's even more important to get everything out of the open.

"You never want to go into attack mode, but when you're feeling insecure [based on their actions], you also don't want to hold in and let it fester," she says. "The emotional pressure cooker that this creates will explode if you do so, and the results won't be pretty."

Be super transparent about what is bothering you and why to prevent this whole mess.

Is Flirting a Cheating Form?

Maybe your partner has a flirty personality, and the second you see them chatting to another person, you go into the worst-case-scenario mode. "What one person often considers flirting, the other regards friendliness," notes Squyres.

She suggests explaining how each of you sees the difference

between flirting and friendliness — or whatever discrepancy you may encounter — then discuss what you're willing to change.

4. Concentrate on the positive attributes.

If you don't love yourself, how do you love someone else in the h*ll? I know, said more easily than done. No one (not even the most confident drag queen) becomes an overnight self-loving master-you have to start small.

Orbuch recommends making a list of five things you like about yourself and then reading them whenever you start to feel in doubt about yourself.

Make a list of your unique gifts while you are at it, too, she says. Perhaps you're doing Instagram-worthy acai bowls on the reg or tackling hills like a pro in your cycling class—feast on them, whatever your talents.

5. Build up those wins.

Building on your self-confidence in one area of your life that is already going well — work, for instance — is a fabulous way to boost your overall self-image.

Whatever you like about yourself as an individual can translate into your relationship, helping you to overcome your insecurities as a partner,

After all, if you believe you're a total catch (which, btw, you 're ARE), then your other half will.

6. Don't compare to others.

Oh, Instagram: The inspiration apex AND insecurity. The social media platform makes instant self-doubt all too easy to trigger, mostly because it can cause you to compare your life (with all its ups and downs) to the highlight reel of someone else.

Remember: The most common insecurity people bring in relationships is feeling "not enough," But you can't feel like you're "not enough" when you don't have someone to compare to, right?

One (relatively) easy way to halt unfavorable comparisons is to take a break from social media, even if it's just a few hours or days. Or reduce your overall use of social media. (Gasp)

Cutting back on scrolling will help you reset expectations for yourself and your relationship, and most importantly, those expectations will be based on your actual desires and needs, not on how you * * think * * measure up to others.

If you're still in a "she's X," they have Y mindset, consider muting or unfollowing people that spike that negative rabbit hole of comparison.

Then go back to your talent list, or create one that spells out all the things you're grateful for in your life, so you're not only forced to leave the app, but you also remember that there's no one like you — I repeat, nobody.

7. Converse with a professional.

Real talk: Even if you've got the world's most supportive partner, sometimes you just have to get help from outside. Your history can result in insecurities, yes, but also just your general personality, Squyres says. "Some people are more anxious, more compulsive, more ruminant, or more self-conscious than others."

So if you've put in all of the above work and still don't feel better, it might be time to speak with a therapist or coach; you can then set goals together and figure out strategies to change.

THINGS YOU NEED TO DO BEFORE SEEKING FOR COUPLES COUNSELING

Even interacting with a therapist will help you see your insecurities in a different light.

Perhaps you have already figured out, for example, that the root cause of your insecurity is a betrayal from a past partner. You're afraid that your current partner will do the same, but you don't necessarily want to tell them this.

Having an unbiased person, like a therapist or coach, listen to your concerns and immerse yourself in them can help you find connections that you wouldn't have if you just went to a nodding friend.

Finally, take heart in knowing that "a good relationship built on love, respect, communication, and commitment should help most people lose their insecurity," Squyres says.

And remember this: You will discover a degree of trust that you might not have found on your own when people just remember your faults and love you anyhow.

CHAPTER 5

ANXIETY AND DEPRESSION

Disorders of anxiety are also related to depression. Both conditions must be dealt with at the same time.

People with anxiety disorders — a disease of social anxiety, generalized anxiety disorder, obsessive-compulsive disorder — or phobias spend most of their time in an anxious condition.

That can take an enormous emotional toll after a while, and depression sometimes sets in. According to the Anxiety and Depression Association of America, there's no definitive reason as to why anxiety and depression coexist so much. Still, you will receive relief from both with the right care.

Which Anxiety Conduces Depression

Anxiety disorders are far more than simple nervousness and anxiety. They can trigger fear of things other people wouldn't give a second thought to. Many people with anxiety disorders realize that they have irrational beliefs, but they still cannot avoid them.

"It's a circle," says Sally R. Connolly, LCSW, a therapist with Louisville's Couples Therapy in Kentucky. "You seem to get this omnipresent anxiety about some concern or some problem when you get nervous, and you feel bad about it. Then you feel like you have failed, and you fall into depression."

The relation between the two conditions is complicated:

In addition to an anxiety disorder, the likelihood of experiencing depression is high-about half of all people with significant depression often suffer from extreme and recurrent anxiety.

"People who are depressed also feel stressed and nervous, so one can cause another," she says. "Too often, anxiety comes before depression."

Both depression and other anxiety disorders may have a biological predisposition.

According to the National Institute of Mental Health (NIMH), people with post-traumatic stress disorder (PTSD), an anxiety disorder, are particularly likely to experience depression too.

"There is always a family background, particularly with anxiety, more so than depression, and so we think there might be a genetic predisposition to that," Connolly explains. "Most people just stress and move it on."

Symptoms of Depression and Anxiety

These are symptoms a person can suffer from an anxiety disorder as well as depression:

- Constant, unreasonable anxiety and fear

- Physical symptoms, such as rapid heartbeat, fatigue, hot flashes, nausea, abdominal pain, headaches, and breathing difficulty

- Ignorance

- Changes in food, too much or too little

- Remembrance, decision making and concentration difficulties

- Constant feelings of sadness or futility

- Hobbies and hobbies lost interest

- Feeling tired and nauseous

- Inability to unwind

- Blows of fear

The Road to Recovery

One should treat both anxiety and depression together. Successful treatment methods include:

- Cognitive-behavioral therapy (CBT) which is commonly used to treat depression anxiety disorder. CBT can teach people how to handle their anxiety, anxieties, and depressive symptoms by finding out what triggers them; people can also learn how to control their emotions.

- Medicinal antidepressants, which can be used to help with both conditions. Often these medications are used in combination with CBT. According to the NIMH, selective serotonin reuptake inhibitors (SSRIs) are newer, commonly used antidepressants that provide fewer side effects than older antidepressants.

- An exercise can also benefit both anxiety and depression disorders. Exercise releases hormones that make you feel good in your body, which can help you relax. The Anxiety and Depression Association of America notes that taking only a 10-minute walk can relieve the symptoms for several hours.

- Relaxation techniques include meditation and awareness practice. According to a broad research review published in the March 2014 issue of JAMA Internal Medicine, both can relieve the symptoms of both anxiety and depression and improve the quality of life.

- Organizations are providing mental health programs that can include in your community a hospital or support group. Check out America's National Center of Mental

Health for more information, or the Anxiety and Depression Association.

You shouldn't ignore warning signs

Those who deal with anxiety and depression should look for these warning signs of a mental health crisis:

- Inadequate everyday self-care, such as denying personal hygiene practices, getting out of bed, or eating

- Severe and sudden mood shifts

- Getting angry, dangerous, or aggressive

- Substances Misuse

- Looks lost or has hallucinations

- Thinking about suicide or finding no reason to live

Treatment for anxiety and depressive disorders needs to be administered and handled by a doctor, says Connolly. "Having a clear evaluation to rule out bipolar disorder is especially important for people with both [anxiety and depression]," she said. Bipolar disorder, a disease in which emotions may range from very low to very high levels of mania and depression, is treated with depression much differently from an anxiety disorder.

No one, and not both, has to suffer from anxiety disorder or depression. People with anxiety disorder should talk about their symptoms with a doctor, therapist, or other health care provider and seek therapy before depression has an opportunity to set in.

How advice will help you to control your anxiety

Anxiety is the number one reason to seek clinical help. Anxiety is on a continuum, and the symptoms can range from everyday anxiety to a persistent sense of distress and even full-blown panic attacks.

If anxiety becomes a concern for you, then therapy will help you control your symptoms and improve your anxiety relationship.

Anxiety, however, is just as much a social problem as a personal one. We are living in a world full of restrictions, aspirations, and responsibilities. So if you go for high-anxiety treatment, the first step is to make you understand that your anxiety is part of a broader social picture in which you work and, second, the deep-dated.

Your anxiety is also a symptom of something else: depression, morbid fears, or problems of identity.

The desire to monitor people and events in your life is what lies at the heart of the anxiety. If absolute control is not feasible, then everything fails here. Anxiety, with its worst-case – panic attacks – comes with a sense of not being a safe place for the planet. Thus, a therapy room may become an island of protection and peace, which in itself is healing.

Anxiety is also commonly correlated with the "good girl / good boy" mentality and perfectionism. Here a therapist can help you become conscious of and note your repetitive behavior patterns in your daily life. When you start to know the habits, they don't get scared anymore, and the burden is released. Learning how to ask for support and embrace it becomes an invaluable new ability.

You may see your anxiety as something in your mind that takes over your thought: "Why can't I stop thinking about it? "I can't stop worrying." If you recognize your thoughts there, then it can be helpful for you to work with a therapist who uses techniques to get you into your body, feelings, and emotions. These techniques may include visualization, working parts, sand tray, working cards, writing a letter to your body, or emotion journaling. The goal of this work is to achieve "grounding": to make you feel safe, relaxed, and focused once more. The purpose of therapy is to help you get out of the ever-worrying mind world and to learn the new skills of being in the present, not in the past or future.

While everybody may be anxious from time to time for various reasons, people usually seek counseling support when they feel their anxious thoughts or state is beginning to impact on their overall health, relationships, or life.

Counseling will also help people with anxiety by doing the following:

1. Offer yourself a supportive relationship and a healthy atmosphere, and share your true feelings without bias or judgment.

2. Encourage self-consciousness to recognize the context and causes of the anxiety.

3. Establish a holding room where you can work through your problems. It can also include a new prism through which you can start looking at your problems from another, yet healthier viewpoint.

4. Empower yourself to help reduce or resolve your feelings of anxiety (including mindfulness and CBT exercises) through the application of various therapeutic strategies/ techniques.

5. Provide practical tools and support to help foster a sense of agency and control within you in achieving its goals

6. Ultimately, therapy will make you feel less burdened and develop a sense of freedom to live your life optimally by conversation and active listening.

CHAPTER 6
THE NEGATIVE EFFECTS OF ANXIETY ON INTIMATE RELATIONSHIPS

The substance of pop songs and poetry has long been the wonder, fear, and curiosity that is so much a part of meeting somebody new: what are they doing right now? Do they want to think about me? But once a bond is formed, and two lives merge, such anxieties are typically replaced by the comforts and intricacies of understanding and trusting one's partner and of, yes, even some form of predictability and routine. But when such thoughts are not tempered by a large, healthy view of one's own life, they can start to take over, unleashing a powerful and destructive emotional force that can have catastrophic consequences for both partners.

Naturally, individuals look to their intimate partners for physical closeness. They seek their consolation or help; they may rely on them, and a separation saddens them. During infancy, the defining features of an individual's attachment to their caregivers may affect the way they perceive intimate relationships.

Appendix Theory Explained

According to British psychologist John Bowlby's theory of attachment, the quality of care received during infancy, including sensitivity and responses to a child's signals, affects the nature of an individual's attachment later on in life. The perceptions of parents and other sources of attachment and their ideas affect the internal working model, which is the mental representation of self or themselves and others by a person.

Research with children by the psychologist Mary Ainsworth endorsed Bowlby's claims by suggesting three distinct patterns of attachment: stable, anxious-avoiding, and anxious-ambivalent.

- Securely attached children feel confident that their carers will meet their needs; they feel comfortable exploring new environments, and they have faith in others.

- Anxious-avoiding children perceive their caregiver as indifferent and insensitive, so they do not tend to be distressed to avoid dealing with a caregiver who is rejecting them.

- Anxious-ambivalent children are handled by carers who are often incoherent and erratic. They continue to assume that the only way to get attention and closeness is to exaggerate their expression of discomfort; when separated from their caregivers, they begin to become highly distressed and exhibit trouble moving away from them in discovering new surroundings.

THE SYMPTOMS OF ANXIETY

Individuals who are anxiously attached appear to experience more extreme negative emotional responses and cognitions, such as rumination and downplay, and deny positive life events and experiences. Findings from a study studying individuals with a social anxiety disorder and attachment types found that those with nervous attachment reported more extreme social anxiety and avoidance, greater disability, higher depression, and lower life satisfaction than participants with a stable attachment.

Anxiously Attached Adult and Romantic Relationships

Stable adults are known for having optimistic feelings regarding interpersonal relationships while considering the influence of adult commitment on romantic relationships, and they are not afraid of closeness. By comparison, avoiding adults can become uncomfortable if someone comes too close, pretending to be independent and having no one. Anxious adults are clingy types and sometimes feel jealousy; they usually worry a lot about their partner being rejected, so they try to impress and win their approval.

Fear of infidelity may become an overarching concern for those anxiously attached. In a recent study, anxiously attached participants showed themselves to be more hypervigilant regarding their partners' rejection signals, and more likely to interpret certain behaviors—sexual, romantic, and causal interactions—as cheating.

Fears of infidelity and breakup may also affect the actions ("mate preservation behaviors") of adults seeking to minimize the likelihood of infidelity and the relationship breakdown. Findings from a study in 2016 found that women and men who score higher in nervous romantic attachment display more frequent behaviors in partner retention.

Holding Friends in Partnership

Men appear to exhibit such behaviors more often, and in general, they scored higher on tests showing nervous romantic commitment than women. From an evolutionary perspective, it could make sense to increase the frequency of mate retention behaviors because the specter of cuckoldry and ambiguous paternity was an important problem for men. Men registered higher scores on behaviors such as direct guarding, vigilance, time monopolizing, envy-inducing, punishing a partner's threat of infidelity, manipulation of emotions and loyalty, negative acts, aggression against rivals, obedience and degradation, and public signals of ownership. In comparison, women seem to use a distinct range of mate retention strategies — meaning to improve their beauty, affection, and care.

ANXIETY IN CLOSE RELATIONSHIPS

While much of this discussion focuses on the aspects of anxious attachment to the self, it is not difficult to find a relationship that is impaired by this problem. Many individuals who are anxiously attached may appear clingy, controlling, or even aggressive. Their anxieties reflect their over-dependence for support and reassurance on their partner — to give a meaning and intent of their lives.

Paradoxically this puts a strain on relationships and leads to lower satisfaction in relationships.

And while this type of attachment slices through the fabric of one's most intimate connections a damaging course, the termination of such a relationship does little to relieve the situation. People who are anxiously attached will respond to break-ups with angry protests, an all-consuming obsession with the former partner, a heightened sexual attraction to win back the individual, and often self-medicating with alcohol or drugs.

CHAPTER 7
THE PURPOSE OF RELATIONSHIPS

It seems like most men and women are chasing the dream of finding a perfect partner, falling in love, and living happily ever after. The proof of this? Well, you don't have to look too far to see the vast number of dating agencies, chat rooms, the columns of 'looking' or 'lonely hearts' in papers and magazines, the ever-increasing number of dating TV programs, and the rows and rows of 'How to' books of relationships.

What are the individuals looking for out of a relationship? What should it be for them to figure out? What is it that should create? Without adding the complexities of a relationship, is there not enough going on in their lives? Why can't they be bothered to work at it while they're in a relationship, or spend time and energy in fixing problems, giving up, and moving on to another toxic relationship?

Why?

A relationship's intent may be as simple as providing an atmosphere to raise children in. Recommended. That doesn't clarify the people who don't want to have kids, but who wants to be in a relationship, though?

Why don't people just live alone or with friends, and be happy with that? It's not that easy, after all – doesn't it save the heart from being broken again and again? Being single means you don't have to feel insecure, compromise, fight about little things. Being single means being free to do whatever you want, at the drop of a hat anytime you want to.

Where does it start, this desire to be in a relationship, and to live happily ever after?

- Is it a fundamental longing for love and security?

- Is it a genetic imperative to build an opportunity to have babies and pass on the reservoir of genes?

- Are we, as human beings and as social creatures, supposed to be part of a pair, and does it come back to being part of a pair to be pro-creative?

- Want to do so, so we can?

- Is being in a relationship what our culture, our society, and our family expect of us?

- Is the relationship's intention to make us feel 'happy' – whatever that's normal, so we don't stick out as being 'single?'

- Is there a relationship that should make us feel complete?

What do individuals think it would do for them to be in a relationship?

They'll make them happy, and somehow complete. And the ever-increasing rate of divorce testifies to unfulfilled desires and failure to work things out.

- Others expect a friendship to relieve their deep sense of isolation.

- Others say it is up to their partners to make them happy.

- Others expect their needs (as they perceive them) to be met in a relationship.

- Others believe it is going to make them feel loved and appropriate. Usually, the thought goes something like "if he/she wants to be with me, then I have to be right."

- Some believe "if I'm in a relationship, anything else will be figured out in my life" As if being in a relationship is like a magic wand which has a positive effect on all aspects of your life. It will fix all my problems.

- Others go into a partnership to make it a very different world than one in which they grew up. A new, improved model that works better.

- Many have an idea of how their partner should love them, act, cook, housekeep, raise children, entertain, and care for them.

- Others plan to maintain the partnership financially. Getting a comfortable big house with all mod drawbacks, the new car, lavish holidays, and exciting social experience.

THE SOURCE OF ASSUMPTIONS ABOUT RELATIONSHIPS

Histories, romance novels, television, families, nursery rhymes, movies, magazines, newspapers, cartoons, a family of your own, songs, ballads, fairy tales, myths, legends, etc.

The perceptions of most individuals rely on a young age on what they are related to, the relationship-wise. The relation is made on a level beyond their consciousness. However, this implicit link becomes the strongest possible catalyst for the relationship sense.

Anything like this could go on the link...

Because of whatever situation the child is in, 'she' can relate to a character like Cinderella. And as the story goes, Cinderella enjoyed meeting her prince and lived happily ever after. 'He' might be interacting with Prince Charming. The prince whose so charming, powerful, the hero who's saving and doing it all right.

The presence of that innocent link has far-reaching implications. 'She' will continue, even as an adult, with the implicit hope that an outsider will save her from her condition. This puts pressure on the male to turn everything from 'rags' into 'riches' in her life. 'He,' on the other hand, needs to have a beautiful maiden by his side, be hailed as a hero, be praised for all his successes, and be cared for in-house. Maybe. This is a generalization of enormity. Or it is.

The habits aren't always good, and when recognized, they can come as quite a shock.

Patterns are formed by studying the child's external relationships. The unintentionally occurring role modeling later sets the standards for relationships. History repeats itself several times, no matter how much the person wishes not to repeat what happened to his/her parents. Unfortunately, even more than once.

After the initial lovey-dovey, desire, infatuation, most relationships do something to please point, consist of blame, assumptions, anger, and unfulfilled desires and claims, lack of confidence, communication, and intimacy.

Despite the initial euphoria of being in love, very curious. Soon she learns he isn't charming her prince. Being in love hasn't solved all her problems with herself; in fact, he hasn't rescued her from all the other problems in her life. On the contrary, in her mind, by not supplying her with what she wanted, he has simply added to them, and she has to nag him just to get the lawn finished.

He, on the other hand, feels let down too. His fair maiden is no match for his imagination. She doesn't respect or compliment him. She even puts him down in bed. He enjoys a hero's adulation. He has never been thanked, let alone appreciated for things he does for her and around the house. All he gets is relentless criticism, her voice playing in his head telling him what a let down he's, he's expected to know what to do and when and why he's not a mind reader.

Too many games are played to believe one's life is under balance. Typically such games are played in the name of love. Typically running patterns are therefore dependent and possessiveness. Lots of people feel strong in attempting to manipulate another. Typically, however, this control or superiority over another is short-lived. And so it returns to square one. For someone else to take over and conquer. Maybe that person will leave too. Often alone.

Why should you place the responsibility on another person for your personal development? Do you want them to be both your counselor and your lover?

To become the kind of person that you want to be with.

Like attracts. If you're very emotionally demanding, you're likely to find a partner who has the same needs as you. And you end up with a scenario where you want your needs to be met, and your partner may not be able to satisfy them because they have the same need and want you to satisfy theirs. If there is really good communication, it can become a situation of no-win. When you think of the kind of person you want to spend the rest of your life with, are you like who guy? If your response is no, then the odds are stacked against you.

Like attracts. You know your strengths and weakness when you are content with yourself, you take responsibility for your attitude and behavior, you act from an adult viewpoint rather than from a child viewpoint, and you discover a life purpose.

Think about the qualities you're looking for and think about how you can build those up inside yourself. So is your companion when you are positive and compassionate. So does your partner when you respect yourself.

The Partnership functions when the relationship's intention is not to have another person who could complete you, but to share your fullness with them.

The object of a relationship may be for companionship. Maybe what we are looking for in a relationship is a sharing of the self that is not possible elsewhere. A profound sense of love and connection. An appreciation of who we are really, warts and all (after acknowledging our warts). Maybe we want to be identified in the way our parents used to know us.

A partnership based on common beliefs and interests can be supportive, imaginative, and motivating. It can bring peace, affection, comfort, laughter, happiness, and a haven. It can provide a very positive way of providing a forum for personal development and contribution to society.

A partnership lets you understand and enjoy the differences that make you special. How different an approach from wanting to make your partner like you exactly to the point of washing the dishes, hoovering, walking, etc.

Relationships are precious because they offer a wonderful opportunity for life to build and generate a magnificent experience of who you want to be with your ideas.

A satisfying relationship may provide your children with a supportive atmosphere. When you think about it, that's going to have a big effect. Based on you being a good role model, your kids will then replicate the model for their kids, and so on.

Examples of goals that can last a lifetime and keep the relationship new and enjoyable are: contribute to the health and well-being of those around you; contribute to the financial prosperity of others; contribute to ending hunger on the planet; contribute to ending tension in people's lives; solve the world's problems of violence, abuse or poverty, etc.

Nice, optimistic, safe, and meaningful relationships give us the richest experiences we can have. Your caring partner who shares everything with you; the best friend who interacts as few others do with you; the people at work who support you and motivate you to become the best you can be; this is what brings joy to life!

CHAPTER BONUS
HOW TO RECOVER FROM A TOXIC
RELATIONSHIP

F ew things sound as refreshing as leaving a genuinely toxic bond. The relentless criticism, continuous confrontation, and emotional abuse are such a relief to escape. But what if you find out you took the poison with you?

Unfortunately, the toxicity of bad relationships, like a "gift that keeps on giving" (in the worst of ways) long after the relationship is over, most frequently outlasts the relationship itself. You may find that an emotionally manipulative parent's harsh voice has been internalized, and now your self-talk holds the same messages and tone as your parents did. Perhaps you find that the harsh assumptions of your ex-spouse have colored your relationship with your new partner. Or you could have left a partner for gas lighting, only to find that you still question what your senses and instincts tell you.

And decades later, the patterns we witness and the negative messages we hear can be sticky, stuck to our psyches, and continue to influence us. The longest hostages in abusive relationships are also our minds.

But that doesn't mean that we can never be free entirely. In my practice as a clinical psychologist, I've seen hundreds of individuals manage to liberate their minds from their past relationships. Although the job is never easy or quick, it can be immensely satisfying. In the final step of emancipation, the following concepts can be very beneficial.

• Be careful with yourself. Bear in mind that retraining the brain takes time. You are a career in progress. Messages you have sent can be extraordinarily long-lived during childhood. Even if your toxic relationship was in adulthood and relatively brief, it could be challenging to break the habits you learned. When you learn that the harmful association continues to color your thoughts and emotions, grant yourself compassion. The unhealthy voice is only reinforced by being impatient with yourself; instead, give yourself the time and space required to recover.

Note the way you are talking to yourself. Be on the lookout for what your internal speech tells you. Be curious, like a scientist, as you discover your mind's patterns. The ideas you find must be written down. In reality, with pen and paper, getting the thoughts out of your mind is far more productive than just mentally noticing them. To begin learning more useful ways of thinking, you'll be in a much better place.

Adopt a more gentle voice. Start to substitute more positive ones for your harsh, critical feelings. Not sure what I'm going to say? Just imagine how you'd chat with a dear friend or a kid of your own. Practice consciously using this gentle answer when you catch the old way of speaking to yourself. For example, if you're making a dumb mistake, substitute, "You're such an idiot!" "with," They all make mistakes. What will you learn for next time from this one?

• Lead with compassion. To practice self-kindness, don't wait until you catch the harsh internal expression. Instead, when you reprogram your mind, be positive. In the morning, begin training your thoughts before your feet even hit the floor. Write down three ideas that you want to reinforce and leave them on your table at the bedside. When you wake up, before you get out of bed, read and repeat those thoughts to yourself. You might, for instance, practice thoughts like, See what occurs when you fill your head with emotions that serve you well, "I'm enough to face whatever this day brings." (Adapted from CBT's The Deck.)

• Find your courage. Do more of the tasks that keep you alive, the things you love and are good at. You might have given up these things during your dysfunctional relationship because deceptive individuals usually don't want to see you succeed. A useful antidote to seeing yourself as vulnerable or incompetent is experiencing your competence.

Embracing who you are. Toxic relationships often lead us to conceal essential parts of ourselves or to reject them. For instance, if you were naturally exuberant, you may have been guided to bury the joyful part of yourself by a frequently critical parent. Find quiet moments to listen to what longs to be shared. Look inside for impulses that could squash you. For more of your experience, start to make room.

• Be where you are. Toxic relationships can lead you not only to feel bad about who you are but about even current ones, as though you don't have the right to take up any room at all. But nothing to apologize for is your existence. Since the world has seen fit to welcome your presence, you have a right to be here. Don't want to shrink your body from being where you are, or justify yourself. Stand strong, unapologetically, in the room, you occupy. They're yours. Say the words to yourself as you breathe in, "I Am." As you exhale, say to yourself, "Here." Exactly where you belong.

Finally, take heart; your mind will once again be yours with focus and practice. In the method, each time you grab the old patterns, count it a win. The fact that you note them implies that you are learning, that you are developing, and that you are coming home to yourself.

The Purpose of Our Emotions'

In how we think and act, emotions can play a significant role. The feelings we experience every day will cause us to take action and affect our decisions, both large and small, about our lives. It is essential to understand the three critical components of emotion to truly understand feelings.

An emotion has three parts:

1. A subjective aspect (how the emotion is experienced)

2. A physiological element (how the body reacts to the feeling)

3. An expressive part (how you act in response to your feelings).

In the function and intent of your emotional responses, these distinct elements may play a role.

Emotions, such as a burst of irritation at a co-worker, maybe short-lived or long-lasting, such as sustaining sorrow over a relationship's loss. But why do we experience emotions, exactly? What position are they serving?

Emotions can encourage us to take measures

You will experience a lot of anxiety when faced with a nerve-wracking exam about whether you will do well and how the test will affect your final score. You might be more likely to study because of these emotional answers. You had the drive to take action and do something constructive to increase your chances of having a good grade because you encountered a specific emotion.

To experience positive feelings and decrease the risk of experiencing negative emotions, we also prefer to take these actions. For instance, you could search for social activities or hobbies that offer you a sense of pleasure, contentment, and excitement. On the other hand, circumstances that might lead to boredom, frustration, or anxiety, you would avoid.

Emotions assist us in living, succeeding and escaping danger

The naturalist Charles Darwin claimed that emotions adapt to survival and reproduction in both humans and animals. We are likely to confront the root of our frustration when we are upset. We are more likely to escape the danger when we feel fear. We could look for a mate and reproduce when we feel love.

In our lives, emotions play an adaptive role by inspiring us to act quickly and take actions that increase our chances of survival and achievement.

Emotions will assist us in making decisions

From what we decide to have for breakfast to what candidates we want to vote for in political elections, our feelings have a big impact on our decisions. Researchers have also found that individuals with certain brain injury levels that impair their capacity to perceive emotions also have a diminished ability to make good choices.

Even in conditions where we think our choices are driven solely by logic and rationality, feelings play a crucial role. In decision making, emotional intelligence, or our ability to recognize and control emotions, has been shown to play an important role.

Emotions help other individuals to recognize us.

It is essential to provide clues when we communicate with other individuals to understand how we feel. Via body language, such as different facial expressions associated with the specific emotions we feel, these signals can include emotional expression.

It could mean specifically stating how we feel in other situations. We send them valuable details when we tell friends or family members that we feel happy, sad, excited, or afraid, which they can then use to take action.

Emotions Help Us Understand Others

Much as our feelings provide others with useful information, we are provided a wealth of social information by those around us' emotional expressions. Social communication is an integral part of our everyday lives and relationships, and it is necessary to understand and respond to others' emotions.

It enables us to respond appropriately to our friends, family, and loved ones and develop more profound, more meaningful relationships. It also helps us connect efficiently in several social contexts, from interacting with an unhappy client to handling a hot-headed employee.

One of the first scholars to study emotions scientifically was Charles Darwin. Emotional displays may also play an essential role in protection and survival, he suggested. It would clearly show that the creature was angry and defensive if you met a hissing or spitting animal, causing you to back off and escape the potential threat.

Understanding others' emotional displays gives us a good insight into how we would need to respond in a specific situation.

Our emotions serve a wide range of purposes, as you have discovered. Fleeting, constant, intense, complex, and even life-changing emotions can be. They can inspire us to behave in specific ways and give us the support and resources we need to engage in our social environments in a meaningful way.